to

_____

from

_____

date

_____

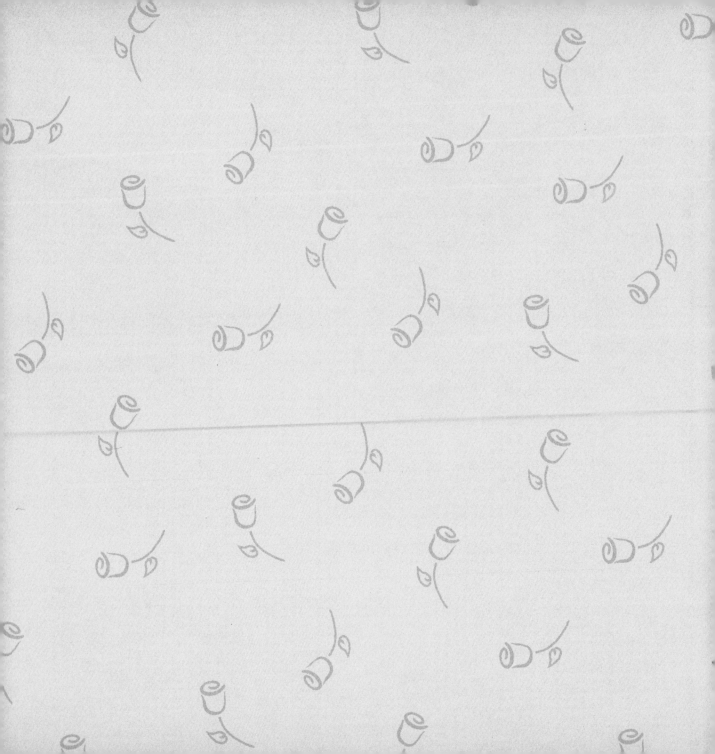

Sugar and Spice

and everything nice

Chrys Howard

PHOTOGRAPHY BY STACI ALBRITTON

HOWARD
®PUBLISHING CO.

dedication

to my sisters, Joneal and Jessi—
who shared the journey of girlhood with me

to my daughters, Korie and Ashley, and granddaughters, Sadie, Macy, and Ally—
who let me continue the journey

Our purpose at Howard Publishing is to:

Increase faith in the hearts of growing Christians
Inspire holiness in the lives of believers
Instill hope in the hearts of struggling people everywhere

Because He's coming again!

Published by Howard Publishing Co., Inc.,
3117 North 7th Street, West Monroe, LA 71291-2227

01 02 03 04 05 06 07 08 09 10   10 9 8 7 6 5 4 3 2 1

Interior design by LinDee Loveland
Photo hand tinting by Toni Worsham

Photography by Staci Albritton
Albritton Photography, 410 North 6th Street, West Monroe, LA 71291

Library of Congress Cataloging-in-Publication Data
Howard, Chrys, 1953–
Sugar and spice and everything nice / Chrys Howard ; photography by Staci Albritton.
p. cm.
ISBN 1-58229-162-4
1. Girls—Poetry. 2. Girls—Quotations, maxims, etc. I. Albritton, Staci.
II. Title.
PS3608.O9 S8 2001
811'.6—dc21   2001016708

Scriptures quoted from The Holy Bible, New Century Version, copyright © 1987, 1988, 1991 by Word
Publishing, Dallas, Texas 75234. Used by permission.

What are little boys made of?
What are little boys made of?
Frogs and snails
And puppy-dog tails,
That's what little boys are made of.

What are little girls made of?
What are little girls made of?
Sugar and spice
And all that's nice,
That's what little girls are made of.

Robert Southey, English poet
1774–1843

What are little **girls** made of?

Sugar and spice and everything nice

Sunshine and rainbows

and ribbons and hairbows

Pink candy canes

and new Mary Janes

God made the world with its towering trees,
Majestic mountains and restless seas.
Then paused and said, "It needs one more thing—
Someone to laugh and dance and sing,
To walk in the woods and gather flowers,
To commune with nature in quiet hours."

So God made little girls
With laughing eyes and bouncing curls,
With joyful hearts and infectious smiles,
Enchanting ways and feminine wiles.
And when He'd completed the task He'd begun,
He was pleased of the job He'd done.
For the world when seen though little girl eyes
Greatly resembles Paradise.

AUTHOR UNKNOWN

Little girls are the nicest things that can happen to people.
They are born with a little bit of angel-shine about them
and though it wears thin sometimes, there is always enough left to lasso your heart—
even when they are sitting in the mud, or crying temperamental tears
or parading up the street in mother's best clothes.

DALE EVANS ROGERS

Everything on earth, shout with joy to God!
Sing about his glory! Make his praise glorious!

Psalm 66:1–2

What are little girls made of?

Costumes and schemes

and magical dreams

Music and dance

and taking a chance

A child to hold and cuddle,
'Tis a gift from God above.
And the world is so much brighter,
When you have a child to love.

AUTHOR UNKNOWN

God makes the world all over again whenever a little child is born.

JEAN PAUL RICHTER

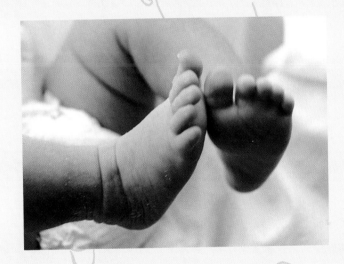

I praise you because you made me in an amazing and wonderful way.
What you have done is wonderful. I know this very well.

Psalm 139:14

What are little **girls** made of?

Ponytails and hats

and swinging a bat

Breezes and butterflies

and raindrops from summer skies

My feet were made to carry me
And how I love to run,
Past the garden and the gate,
Just soaking up the sun.

My hands were made to touch and feel,
Flowers, trees, and such.
I want to say, "Thank you, God,
For giving me so much."

CHRYS HOWARD

Children have neither past nor future;
they employ the present, which very few of us do.

LA BRUYERE

Sing a new song to him; play well and joyfully.

Psalm 33:3

What are little **girls** made of?

Giggles and grins and shopping with friends

Sisters and treats and matching bare feet

I'm not really sure
What I'll grow up to be.
But I know God has my plans—
He's holding them for me.

He's molding and He's shaping,
And I can't wait to see
The kind of person I'll become
And what God has planned for me.

Does He see me in a classroom
Teaching to the young?
Or maybe in a kitchen
Waiting supper to be done?

Does He see me at a hospital
Nursing someone who needs care
Or working in the beauty shop
Styling ladies' hair?

I guess I'll have to wait and see—
It's not as if I mind—
I'll gladly let God guide my steps
And follow close behind.

CHRYS HOWARD

Keep your eyes on the stars and your feet on the ground.

THEODORE ROOSEVELT

He has put his angels in charge of you

to watch over you wherever you go.

Psalm 91:11

What are little **girls** made of?

Tea parties and laces

and baby-doll faces

High heels and hats

and fuzzy kitty cats

God gave me the greatest gift
In life He can bestow;
He granted me a wondrous child,
And I'm to help her grow.

I am to show her happiness,
But not with what to play,
And teach her to express herself,
But not what to say.

I am to guide her thoughts
Yet help her form a will her own
And teach her to have faith in God
And reap what I have sown.

Yes, God gave me the greatest gift
And to Him I now pray,
"Please grant to me the strength I'll need
To watch her walk away."

MARCIA KRUGH LEASER

A child is a beam of sunlight from the Infinite and Eternal,
with possibilities of virtue and vice—
but as yet unstained.

LYMAN ABBOTT

Let our daughters be like the decorated stones in the Temple.

Psalm 144:12

What are little **girls** made of?

Hugs and kisses and holiday wishes

Laughter and love

I have a friend in Jesus
He's the best friend I know.
He walks and talks with me each day
And leads me as I go.
But sometimes I need to see
My Jesus with some skin
It's then I know how blessed I am
That you became my friend.

CHRYS HOWARD

Girls are especially fond of exchanging confidences
with those who they think they can trust;
it is one of the most charming traits of a simple, earnest hearted girlhood,
and they are the happiest women who never lose it entirely.

LUCY LARCOM

This is the day that the Lord has made.
Let us rejoice and be glad today!

Psalm 118:24

What are little **girls** made of?

Warm summer days

and daddies who play

Blankets and bears and sweet good-night prayers

That's what little **girls** are made of.

Each second we live is a new and unique moment
of the universe, a moment that will never be again...
And what do we teach our children?...
We should say to each of them: do you know what you are?
You are a marvel. You are unique.
In all the years that have passed, there has never been another child like you.
Your legs, your arms, your clever fingers, the way you move.
You may become a Shakespeare, a Michelangelo, a Beethoven.
You have the capacity for anything. Yes, you are a marvel.

PABLO CASALS

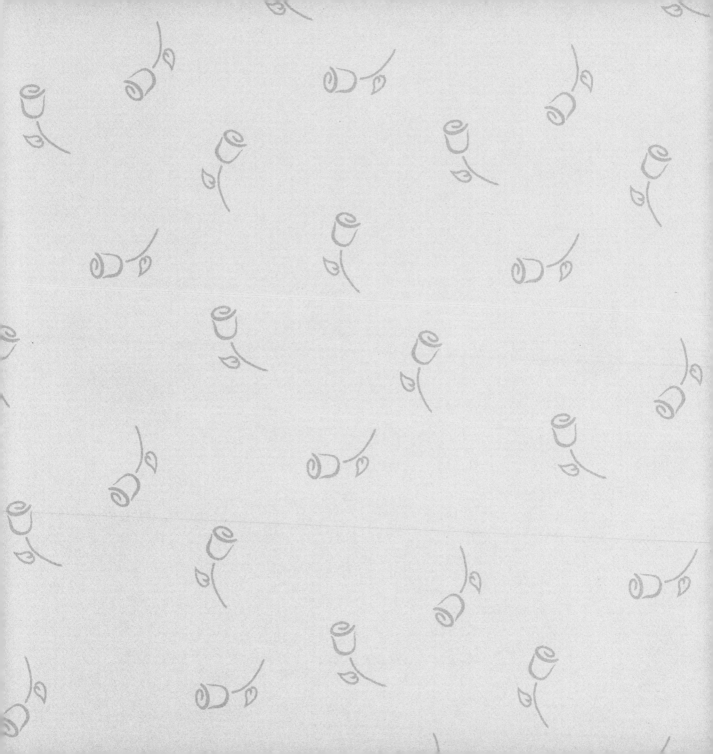